CW00338484

THE PHILOSOPHY OF
TEA

THE PHILOSOPHY OF
TEA

TONY GEBELY

First published 2019 by
The British Library
96 Euston Road
London NW1 2DB

ISBN 978 0 7123 5259 8
eISBN 978 0 7123 6495 9

Cataloguing in Publication Data
A catalogue record for this book is available
from the British Library

Designed and typeset by Sandra Friesen
Printed and bound by Finidr, Czech Republic

CONTENTS

THE JOURNEY BEGINS

'PHILOSOPHY' REFERS to the study of the fundamental nature of knowledge, reality and existence. In this book we're going to explore the philosophy of tea. Yes, tea.

What may at first appear to be a simple beverage has a vast and impressive history, and if you are a consumer primarily of black tea from tea bags, you'll be surprised to learn that the variety of flavours the tea plant is able to produce naturally is difficult to rival even in the world of wine. What is the tea plant, you say? More on that in the next chapter.

Today, tea is the most drunk beverage in the world after water. But it hasn't always been. Tea remained a secret of China's for thousands of years before the lips of a Westerner first touched a cup of it. The invigorating drink drove advancements in shipping, led to the colonisation of now popular tea regions in India by the British, sparked the Opium Wars between Britain and China and was one of many factors that led to the American Revolution. This is the lure of tea—there are so many stories that can be told about a seemingly simple drink made from leaves.

I first experienced tea as a young teenager. Tea was prescribed for me by my mother when I was ill, almost as a sort of panacea, as it was for so many others in the United States. Sore throat, common cold, flu—all such ailments were remedied with a cup of black tea from a tea bag. The perfect companion on a hot summer day was a cold glass of iced tea, also made from black tea bags, with the addition of copious amounts of sugar.

Throughout university, I worked at a cafe as a barista and became more interested in the tea that was sold than the coffee. In 2005 I joined a month-long university trip to China to study the geology of southern China. It was during this trip that my love for tea blossomed, and I realised that there was a world of knowledge about this drink that hadn't yet reached our shores in the West. I read every book on tea I could get my hands on, including classics such as *All about Tea* by William H. Ukers and *The Tea Lover's Treasury* by James Norwood Pratt. Later, in 2008, I ventured back east on a six-month backpacking expedition through Southeast Asia. In 2009 I started my own tea-importing company; in 2011 I met my wife (who was also studying tea); and in 2016 I published my first book on tea, *Tea: A User's Guide*.

From these experiences, I went from being a *tea drinker* to becoming a *tea taster*. Tea became more than a simple beverage for me—I yearned to taste all the teas that I could get my hands on, training my palate as I tried more and more styles of tea. Tea became exciting!

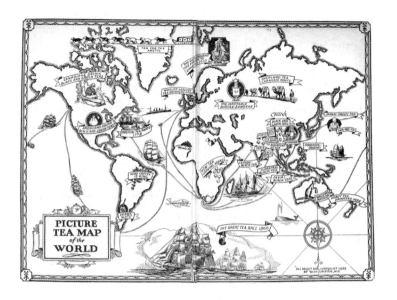

This type of story is what we in the industry call a *tea journey*. Once tea becomes more than a beverage for you, once it grips you, it takes you on a journey. You cannot stop it, and your captivation by it grows as you realise that the more you learn about tea the less you truly know about it. Throughout my tea journey, I have spent months chasing the tea harvest across Asia and have met countless others doing the same, many of whom have become great friends. The simple act of sharing tea with someone bridges cultures, transcending any differences, requiring no common spoken language and fostering friendship.

Throughout this book, we'll find out the various types and styles of tea being produced today, explore tea's dramatic history and look at some of the world's most interesting tea cultures. My hope is that, after reading this book, your eyes will be opened to the huge impact that tea has had on the world we live in today and you will understand what it takes to make a humble cup of tea. And maybe, just maybe, this book will encourage you to take the first steps of your own tea journey.

The most consumed tea in the world is black tea, and rightly so as the majority of the world's tea production is black tea. Over the next few chapters we'll cover five other types of tea as well—products largely of different processing steps that fresh tea leaves undergo.

WHAT IS TEA?

WE KNOW that tea exists. But what does it mean to people aside from being their favourite beverage? For some, it's just that, a beverage, while for others it embodies comfort and relaxation or provides a much needed break in the day. Still others would venture to declare that tea solves all of life's problems.

Let's get back to reality, though. Most of us call any sort of plant matter that we steep in water 'tea'. But to truly be considered tea, the plant matter must be from the varieties and cultivars of the tea plant, nothing other than *Camellia sinensis*.

This means that chamomile tea, hibiscus tea, mint tea, ginger tea, lemongrass tea, rooibos tea and anything else we steep that doesn't come from *Camellia sinensis* aren't really teas at all. We call these other plant materials steeped in hot water *tisanes* or *herbals*.

The tea plant, *Camellia sinensis*, is a broad-leaved perennial evergreen tree that is native to East Asia. It's related to the many flowering camellias, most famously *Camellia*

NEWSPAPER ADVERTISEMENTS OF TEA FROM FIVE COUNTRIES

Top row includes specimens of American, German, and British publicity, and second row, British and French. Centre section, American, Chinese, and British. Bottom row, American, British, and Japanese copy.

japonica, that are a favourite of gardeners. To produce tea, *Camellia sinensis* is typically cultivated in rows and pruned waist high so that the newest leaves can be plucked by hand or cut by machine for processing into tea. What we mean by processing is any combination of steps through which the leaves go once they are separated from the plant and which turns them into any one of the six types of tea: green tea, yellow tea, white tea, oolong tea, black tea or fermented tea (we'll explore these a bit more over the next few chapters).

The largest producers of true tea in the world today are China, India, Kenya, Sri Lanka and Turkey. Together these countries account for nearly 80 per cent of the world's tea production.[1] But how did we get to this place where tea producers worldwide are satisfying the thirst of billions? In the rest of this book, we'll explore how tea leaves are transformed by processing and how this beloved crop encircled the globe to become a daily beverage for billions.

SIX TEAS, ONE PLANT

IF ALL TRUE tea comes from the same plant, you may be wondering why there are so many different kinds of tea on the market today and how they can all be so different. In fact, the number of varieties of teas available to us is difficult to match in the worlds of coffee or even wine. You can easily go through life drinking tea every other day and never drink the same tea twice.

There are so many styles of tea available to us for a number of reasons. Let us explore the major causes of differentiation between teas, starting with the processing steps that the tea leaves go through. The greatest effect on the outcome of a tea is the result of *tea processing*, which is an umbrella term for a number of ways in which the leaves are manipulated by humans and machines between being picked and reaching your cup. We'll go into more detail about how each tea is made in the next few chapters.

The second most important reason for the myriad of tea styles available to us is the variety or cultivar of *Camellia sinensis* that is used to make the tea. Just as there are many

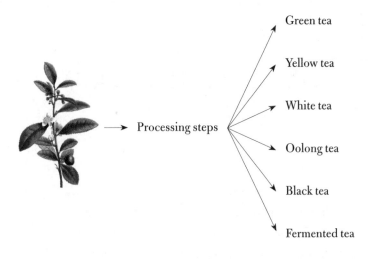

Green tea

Yellow tea

White tea

Processing steps → Oolong tea

Black tea

Fermented tea

varieties of apples available on the market (e.g., Cox, Gala, Golden Delicious), different varieties and cultivars of tea plants produce teas that taste different.

The care given to the plants as they grow and the location where they are grown (known as *terroir*, or taste of place) also affect the outcome of a tea. This is why a tea from China tastes different from one produced in India, even though they may have been processed in a similar way. All sorts of factors influence *terroir*, such as weather, the minerals in the soil, air quality and climate.

Tea can also be altered after processing with flavours or additives, resulting in many more thousands of styles of tea. An example of an altered black tea is the famous Earl Grey, a black tea flavoured with bergamot oil.

General

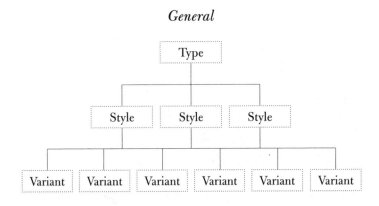

Specific

It's helpful to think of tea in terms of a hierarchy. There are six *types* of tea: green tea, yellow tea, white tea, oolong tea, black tea and fermented tea. Think of these types as clusters of teas made in a similar manner. Individual teas within these clusters may differ slightly and have their own style. Tea *styles* have undergone similar processing steps and exhibit similar characteristics, but with a few differences, such as origin, cultivar, slight variations in processing or differences in additives for altered teas. For example, there are hundreds of styles of black tea—Dian hong from China, Nuwara Eliya from Sri Lanka and Assam from India, to name just a few.

Today, most cultivated tea plants are grown in rows and pruned to about waist high for ease of harvest. Depending

A TEA GARDEN.—The Tea plant flourishes best in the provinces of To-kien, Kiang-su, Hoonam and Hoopels. The first crop is gathered in the early spring.

upon the socio-economic forces at play in the country of production, tea leaves are either plucked from the plant by hand or harvested by machine before being processed. Most processing today is mechanised, though some artisan producers still process teas by hand. As you might imagine, teas that are produced by hand can be quite expensive!

Nearly all of the processing steps used in tea production around the world today originated in China. This is why parts of the book may seem to focus rather a lot on China. Tea was produced in China for thousands of years before it was commercially produced elsewhere, and today China produces 35 per cent of the world's tea,[2] so we owe our thanks to the Chinese for our beloved cuppa.

The methods of tea processing that have been developed over several thousand years enable tea producers to control the natural breakdown of the tea leaves once they have been removed from the plant. Careful manipulation (or prevention) of this breakdown is what differentiates tea types from one another. One of the most important chemical reactions that is controlled by the steps in tea processing is oxidation. Consider an example of oxidation from outside the tea world: when you cut an apple, it begins to turn brown, and if you heat it the inside remains white and does not turn brown. Heat is applied to tea leaves in the same way to prevent oxidation, which is why green tea leaves are still green when we buy them and black tea leaves are brown.

Let's discuss what makes each tea type unique and explore some of the most famous styles in each type.

GREEN TEA

WE BEGIN our journey through the different types of tea with green tea. This is the most popular type of tea in China, Japan and Morocco, but is overshadowed by the popularity of black tea in the rest of the world.

As we learned in the last chapter, when tea leaves are harvested from the tea plant, they begin to break down naturally. The defining step in green tea processing is the prevention of this breakdown: tea leaves are heated soon after harvesting, a process called *fixing*. Heating the leaves stops the chemical reactions that cause the leaves to oxidise and turn brown. This results in tea leaves that remain green and that retain their fresh vegetal taste.

Oxidation here refers to a number of chemical processes that result in the browning of tea leaves and is best explained by our apple example in the last chapter. The prevention of oxidation is why apples in an apple pie and in apple sauce are not brown, and why tea leaves that have been heated remain green.

Back to our story of green tea: once the tea leaves have been heated, they are shaped or rolled and then dried. The most sought-after green teas are made from tender, young tea leaves.

The method of heating the leaves varies depending on the type of tea being made, but the most common method is to heat the leaves in a hot pan, a process that has recently been mechanised across most major tea-producing regions in China. The most famous green teas from China are long jing, Tai Ping hou kui, and Dong Ting bi luo chun.

In Japan, the primary method of heating the leaves uses steam. Steam stops the browning process more quickly, resulting in leaves that are greener and that exhibit much stronger vegetal notes than those that have been heated in a pan. This steaming process is responsible for the production of many famous Japanese green teas, including sencha, gyokuro, the many regional styles of bancha, and tencha (which is used for the production of matcha). Not all Japanese green teas are steamed, however: kamairicha is a style of green tea that is pan-fired and rolled by hand.

Many people dislike green tea because of its astringency and bitterness. Astringency here refers to the drying sensation on the tongue, which is often associated with bitter things. Nine times out of ten, this unpleasant taste is the result of improperly prepared green tea. It is likely that that drink was prepared using too much tea, that the water was too hot or that the tea was steeped for too long. We'll cover proper tea preparation in a later chapter.

Sencha 煎茶

Sencha, or 'steamed tea', is arguably the most famous style of Japanese green tea. The fresh tea leaves are steamed, rolled and dried, resulting in shiny, dark green, needle-shaped tea leaves. The longer the steaming process, the less pristine the final leaves will be, as the steaming process breaks down the leaf structure.

Gyokuro 玉露

Literally 'jade dew', gyokuro is a steamed Japanese green tea produced in the same fashion as sencha, but the tea plants are shaded for three weeks before being harvested. This shading increases the concentration of amino acids and decreases the concentration of polyphenols in the leaves, resulting in a less astringent tea with a stronger umami (savoury) taste.

Matcha 抹茶

Matcha is a style of Japanese green tea made from steamed tea leaves that have been ground into a very fine powder. Literally 'fine powder tea', matcha is a very bright green powder ground in a large granite mill called an *ishiusu*. Matcha is often produced in two grades, ceremonial grade and ingredient grade. The major difference between matcha and other teas (apart from its being ground into a powder) is that it is typically prepared using a whisk to create a suspension of tea powder in hot water.

Xi Hu Long Jing 西湖 龙井 (xī hú lóng jǐng)

Literally 'West Lake dragon well', Xi Hu long jing is arguably the most famous style of Chinese green tea, and also appears in the well-known list of ten famous Chinese teas. Authentic long jing is grown in the areas surrounding West Lake in Zhejiang Province's capital, Hangzhou. The leaves are withered in the sun and then finished (fixed, shaped and dried) entirely in the pan. The finished leaves are pale green and flat.

Tai Ping Hou Kui 太平猴魁 *(tà píg hó ku)*

Literally 'Tai Ping monkey king', this style of tea is produced in Tai Ping County in Anhui Province and is one of China's ten famous teas. It is often made from a single bud and two large leaves that are withered, pan-fired, pressed between screens and then baked. The tea is made up of long, pale green, flat-pressed leaves with a chequerboard pattern (from the pressing) that appear fleshy once brewed.

Dong Ting Bi Luo Chun 洞庭碧螺春
(dòng tíng bì luó chūn)

Literally 'Dong Ting green snail spring', this style of tea is grown in the Dong Ting region in Jiangsu Province. To make bi luo chun, the bud and first leaf are plucked from the tea plant and withered. Withering is followed by three processing steps: kill-green, shaping and drying. All three processes are completed by hand in an iron pan or wok. The finished tea is made up of tiny, rolled, hairy green bud sets that resemble green coiled snails. Dong Ting bi luo chun is also one of China's ten famous teas.

YELLOW TEA

YELLOW TEA is rarely produced outside of China, but it is highly regarded. There are entire regions in China dedicated to its production, and its production methods don't resemble those of any of the other five tea types. The production of yellow tea starts off as with green tea, where the leaves are heated soon after harvest, but the leaves are then wrapped in cloth bundles. While wrapped, the leaves turn from green to yellow-green and the vegetal flavours that are common in green tea mellow. The most common styles of yellow tea today are Jun Shan yin zhen, which is made only from the tips of the tea plant, and various regional variations of huang ya.

Jun Shan Yin Zhen 君山银针 *(jūn shān yín zhēn)*
Literally 'Junshan silver needle', this style of tea originated in Junshan Island in Hunan Province. Junshan yin zhen is made up entirely of buds that are fixed, wrapped in small bundles and then dried. This is one of China's ten famous teas, the only yellow tea in the list.

Huang Ya 黄芽 *(huáng yá)*

Literally 'yellow sprout', huang ya is a name given to three famous yellow tea styles: Huo Shan huang ya 霍山黄芽 (huò shān huáng yá), originating in Huoshan County in Anhui Province; Meng Ding huang ya 蒙顶黄芽 (méng dǐng huáng yá), originating in Meng Ding Shan in Sichuan Province; and Mo Gan huang ya 莫干黄芽 (mò gān huáng yá), originating in Mo Gan Shan in Zhejiang Province. Leaves destined to be huang ya are pan-fired to halt oxidation, wrapped in small bundles and then dried.

WHITE TEA

THE PRODUCTION of white tea employs a processing step called withering whereby the tea leaves are allowed to wither for several days before being dried. This withering phase of white tea breaks down compounds in the tea leaves to produce a very strong floral aroma that is evident both in the dry leaves and in a steeped cup of tea. White teas are not rolled or shaped, so the structure of the fresh leaves remains intact in finished white tea.

Fujian Province in China is the home of white tea, specifically the counties of Fuding and Zhenghe. Despite its often being described as such, white tea is not rare, nor is it the most expensive tea. The styles first created in Fujian Province are now being reproduced in nearly all places where tea is grown.

Bai Hao Yin Zhen 白毫银针 *(bái háo yín zhēn)*
Literally 'white hair silver needle', this white tea style is defined by the tiny hairs on the buds that give the tea a silvery-white appearance. This tea originated in the counties of

Fuding and Zhenghe in Fujian Province and is known for its sweetness, as the bud of the tea plant contains energy in the form of sugar to open up into a full bud set. The buds also contain more caffeine than any other portion of the tea plant, mainly for protection against insects. It takes about 10,000 buds to make one kilogram of bai hao yin zhen.[3] To make this tea, buds are withered in the shade for several days and then dried. When it is produced outside China, this style of tea is often given an alternative name, most commonly 'silver tips'.

Bai Mu Dan 白牡丹 *(bái mǔ dan)*

Literally 'white peony', bai mu dan is a style of Chinese white tea that is made of one bud and one or two leaves. To make bai mu dan, the tea leaves are withered for several days and then baked to dry. Bai mu dan is sold in several grades. It is sometimes just labelled as 'bai mu dan', but lower grades of the same tea are also sold as gong mei and shou mei.

OOLONG TEA

OOLONG TEA is, arguably, the most diverse and exciting tea category. Transliterated as 'wulong', which translates as 'black dragon', the tea is far better known as 'oolong'. China and Taiwan are the major producers of oolong in the world today. Oolong tea is made by carefully controlling the natural breakdown of tea leaves once they are removed from the plant and allowing them to oxidise slightly. This is why you will often hear oolong described as being 'in between' green tea and black tea—but, as with many things in the world of tea, it's more complicated than this.

A distinct step in the processing of traditional oolong tea is bruising, where the leaves are shaken and lightly rolled or tumbled until the edges bruise. The bruising causes cellular damage in the leaves and initiates the oxidation process. Bruising as a processing step is an iterative process, wherein the leaves are repeatedly bruised and allowed to wither and oxidise slowly until the tea-maker deems them finished, that is, they have reached the desired level of oxidation. The leaves are then heated (fixed) to stop oxidation, shaped and dried.

An Xi Tie Guan Yin 安溪铁观音 *(ān xī tiě guān yīn)*
Literally 'An Xi iron goddess of mercy', this Chinese tea style is produced in Fujian Province's Anxi County and is arguably the most famous oolong. Tie guan yin is made from the leaves of a cultivar with the same name. Traditional versions of this tea are heavily roasted, but it is most commonly found in a green, unroasted state today. Tie guan yin is one of China's ten famous teas and is known for its floral fragrance and *hou yun* (喉韵), its throat resonance or aftertaste.

Wu Yi Da Hong Pao 武夷大红袍 *(wǔ yí dà hóng páo)*
Literally 'Wu Yi big red robe', this style of Chinese tea is one of the two oolongs (tie guan yin is the other) that make it to the list of ten famous Chinese teas. Da hong pao is the most famous and widely produced Wu Yi oolong tea. This style of tea is famous for its distinctive sweet mellow aftertaste, known as *yan yun* (岩韵), or 'rock rhyme'.

Feng Huang Dan Cong 凤凰单丛 *(fèng huáng dān cōng)*
Literally 'Feng Huang single bush' or 'Feng Huang single trunk', 'dan cong' refers to a style of oolong production where the leaves are plucked and processed from single trees. The original plants were propagated by seed over

700 years ago in the Feng Huang Shan (Phoenix Mountain) region in Guangdong Province in China. The trees are harvested and processed individually, hence the name 'dan cong', or single bush. The tea producers noticed that each plant produced tea that tasted different. Dan cong teas are a perfect example of selective breeding, as many of the plants and resulting teas are named after the fragrance of the finished teas they produced and have since been cloned for commercial production. There are a wide range of dan cong teas from 'honey orchid' to 'duck shit'. It is thought that the name 'duck shit' arose when a farmer didn't want competing farmers to steal cuttings from his tea tree, so he gave his tea an unfavourable name.

Nan Tou Dong Ding 南投 冻顶 *(nán tóu dòng dǐng)*
Arguably the most famous Taiwanese oolong hails from the areas around Dong Ding Mountain in Nantou County in central Taiwan. Fresh leaves destined to become Dong Ding oolong are withered in the sun and then tumbled to bruise the edges of the leaves. This is followed by an iterative process in which the leaves are withered and then further bruised. Once the desired amount of oxidation has been achieved, the leaves are fixed. Once fixed, the leaves are kneaded while wrapped in cloth. The leaf mass forms a tight ball which is then carefully broken apart and kneaded again. This step is responsible for forming the shape of these teas. Once the desired shape is achieved, the leaves

are dried. Dong Ding oolongs are typically produced with lower amounts of roast and oxidation.

Wen Shan Bao Zhong 文山包种 *(wén shān bāo zhǒng)*
Literally 'Wen Shan wrapped kind', bao zhong is a style of oolong from the Wen Shan area of northern Taiwan. Compared to other Taiwan oolongs, bao zhong is typically the least oxidised oolong style, with oxidation levels usually well under 20 per cent. The name 'wrapped kind' comes from an old packaging method where bao zhong leaves were sold wrapped in folded paper. To make bao zhong, the leaves are withered in the sun and then indoors, after which they are lightly tossed to initiate oxidation, rolled and dried.

Dong Fang Mei Ren 东方美人 *(dōng fāng měi rén)*
Literally 'Oriental beauty', this style of tea is also known as bai hao, or white tip oolong from the use of buds in the finished tea. Dong fang mei ren hails from Hsinchu county in northern Taiwan. This tea style is typically heavily withered and heavily oxidised to 70–80 per cent. The oxidation process starts while the leaves are still attached to the plant in the field: when the unsprayed leaves are attacked by jassids (leafhoppers) and other insects, the plant creates more polyphenols to inhibit further insect attack. These polyphenols add complexity and body to the taste of the tea once it is plucked and processed.

BLACK TEA

BLACK TEA is the most widely produced tea type in the world and thus the most consumed. Within the type, lesser-quality broken-leaf black teas—namely fannings and BOP (broken orange pekoe) teas—are the most widely produced and consumed. In fact, most of the famous tea cultures of the world have their basis in cheap black tea, including masala chai of India, Turkish tea, Russian samovar tea and British tea. Black teas have the widest range of sweetness and intensity, ranging from China's Dian hongs, which are sweet and malty and steep up to a beautiful red colour, to India's Assam blacks, which can brew up a liquor brisk and dark enough to require the addition of milk and sugar. This is also the tea type that gives us the breakfast tea style, typically a well-balanced blend of several strong black teas that can take the addition of milk well.

Black teas are often described as being fully oxidised, or more accurately *mostly* oxidised. The basic process for making black tea from fresh tea leaves consists of withering, rolling, oxidation and drying. The goal of black tea production is to induce and control oxidation until the tea leaves achieve a prescribed level of oxidation.

Jin Jun Mei 金骏眉 *(jīn jùn méi)*

Literally 'golden steed eyebrow', jin jun mei is a high-end black tea style from China's Tong Mu Village in Fujian Province consisting solely of buds, which give it a distinctive golden sheen. This tea is produced by leaves that are withered, rolled, allowed to oxidise and dried. As the name suggests, the finished tea is made up of strips of golden-brown leaves.

Qi Men Hao Ya 祁門毫芽 *(qí mén háo yá)*

Qi Men hao ya, literally 'Qi Men downy sprout', is the most common representation of Qi Men (often spelled '*Keemun*'). tea, a black tea from Anhui Province in China. This tea is produced much like the orthodox teas of India—that is, rolled on a rolling table which breaks it up into small, uniform pieces. The finished tea is made up of small pieces of leaves and buds about one centimetre in length.

Darjeeling Black Tea

The Darjeeling region in the Indian state of West Bengal is home to eighty-seven registered tea gardens ranging from 600 metres to 2,000 metres in elevation. These gardens produce several distinct products based on the different flushes or growth periods of the tea plants. First flush

Darjeeling teas are made from the first buds to emerge from the plants in spring and are typically rolled to a lesser degree and are less oxidised (typically to about 35 per cent) than other flushes so as to preserve the fresh nature of the leaves. Many tea aficionados consider first flush Darjeeling teas to be oolongs because of their semi-oxidised nature. Second flush Darjeeling teas are more akin to black teas as they are allowed to oxidise further; they begin with fresh tea leaves which are then withered, rolled, oxidised, dried and sorted. The leaves are broken during the rolling process, and after drying are sorted into grades based on particle size. This is why, though broken, the leaf particles from finished Darjeeling teas are of uniform size. Darjeeling's *terroir* is famous for producing a muscatel flavour, and Darjeeling teas are often called 'the champagne of teas'.

Assam Black Tea

The Assam region is the largest tea production region in India in terms of both size and the amount of tea produced.

There are around 800 tea estates in Assam, most of them at or around sea level. Nearly all of the tea plants grown in Assam are of the Assamica variety of *Camellia sinensis*. There are two methods of initiating oxidation employed in Indian tea manufacture: the orthodox method of rolling and the CTC (crush, tear, curl) method of crushing, tearing and curling the leaves. The production of Assam tea primarily uses the CTC method, where the leaves are withered, macerated using a rotorvane or a CTC machine, allowed to oxidise, dried and then sorted. Finished teas from Assam are notably dark and brisk, as they are primarily produced for blending into breakfast teas, masala blends and other blends that are typically taken with the addition of milk.

Sri Lankan Black Tea
Sri Lanka (known as Ceylon in the days of the British Empire) is the world's fourth largest tea producer, and orthodox black tea accounts for 95 per cent of its total tea production.[4] Sri Lankan tea is categorised by region and elevation. The main production regions are Nuwara Eliya, Dimbula, Kandy, Uda Pussellawa, Uva and Ruhuna, where tea is harvested year-round. The elevation of tea production ranges from near sea level to 1,800 metres above sea level. Tea grown below 600 metres is designated 'low country', that grown between 600 and 1,200 metres is called 'mid-country' and that grown above 1,200 metres is called 'up-country' or 'high country'.

FERMENTED TEA

THE FERMENTED tea category is perhaps the least understood tea category in the West. China is the only major producer of teas in this category, and even there it accounts for only a very small percentage of overall tea production. This category encompasses a wide array of sometimes funky finished tea styles that differ in their raw materials, processing and the shape and size of their leaves. Fermented teas, however, all share a common processing activity—intentional fermentation.

Size may seem an odd way to categorise a tea, but fermented teas are often compressed into shapes. This practice originated in the days when teas were compressed and transported on horseback along the various trade routes in China, most notably the Tea and Horse Road. The Tea and Horse Road is so named as it was used primarily to transport tea bricks from Yunnan Province to Tibet, where they were traded for horses.

There are many regional styles of fermented tea, known as 'hei cha' in Chinese, which translates to 'dark tea', after

the dark colour of the fermented leaves. Heicha is sometimes translated as 'black tea'—but black tea refers to something else that is quite different, so let's keep things simple! Fermented teas vary greatly in size and shape. For example, jin cha is formed into a mushroom shape, jin gua cha is pressed into the shape of a melon and hua juan cha is compressed into a log shape several feet in length and wrapped in woven bamboo, which takes more than one person to carry. But the most famous is Pu'er, a fermented tea from Yunnan Province in China.

Pu'er

Pu'er 普洱 (pǔ ěr) is arguably the most famous fermented tea in the world. Pu'er is often pressed into a disc shape known as a 'cake' (translated from the Chinese *bing*) but is also sold in loose form. Pu'er can be aged, much like a fine wine, where the tea leaves, stored under ideal conditions, are allowed to slowly ferment and oxidise. Tea connoisseurs have begun to collect this tea because of its capacity to age, and this has led to an explosion in the popularity of the tea style and a huge increase in its market price. Widespread speculation as the result of a meteoric rise in the popularity and price of Pu'er saw a tenfold increase in prices between 1999 and 2007. This over-speculation led to a bubble that burst in 2007. Pu'er prices still fluctuate, however, and some regional Pu'er teas remain some of the most expensive teas in China.

To be considered a Pu'er, the tea leaves must be grown in Yunnan Province in China, produced from a large-leaved variety of the tea plant that is indigenous to the region and also dried in the sun. There are two styles of Pu'er: raw (*sheng*) Pu'er and cooked (*shu*) Pu'er. To make either style, tea leaves begin with a firing in a pan and are then rolled and left to dry in the sun. At this point, the leaves can be steamed and pressed into a cake or sold loose—this is sheng Pu'er. Alternatively, the leaves can be force fermented in a large pile—this is shu Pu'er. You may be wondering where the fermentation step for sheng Pu'er is. Sheng Pu'er ferments slowly as it is aged over time; if it is consumed right after production it isn't really fermented tea. This point has led to a contention in the tea world that sheng Pu'er should not be included in the fermented tea (hei cha) category.

Pu'er cakes are wrapped in paper for storage, and these wrappers typically contain information about the provenance of the tea. Lately, tea producers have begun to add striking imagery and artwork to Pu'er cakes, contributing further to the tea's popularity.

THE ORIGIN OF TEA

WHILE WE don't know who first discovered the magical properties of the tea plant, we do know that the tea plant's origin can be traced to a wide swathe of land covering parts of Assam in India, northern Burma and Thailand, Indochina and south-western China.[5] The Chinese are credited with harnessing the power of tea and with making tea what it is today, an unforgettable drink, the most popular beverage on earth aside from water.

The most widespread origin myth for tea dates back to nearly 5,000 years ago in China. The story tells of Shennong, a mythological Chinese deity-ruler who supposedly ruled from 2737 to 2698 BCE, who tasted 100 plants, seventy-two of which made him ill. According to the myth, tea leaves fell into his cauldron of boiling water, and drinking this water cured him of all his ills. However, it is more likely that local people in the area where the tea plant originated chewed the leaves at some point and were impressed by their salubrious effects.

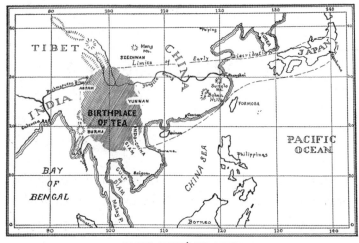

MOTHER NATURE'S TEA-GARDEN

The earliest physical evidence of fresh leaves being processed and made into a beverage was discovered in 2016 in the mausoleum of Emperor Jing of Han in Xi'an China.[6] Chemical and radiocarbon analysis of the leaves showed them to be from *Camellia sinensis* and to date back 2,100 years ago to the Western Han Dynasty (207 BCE–9 CE).

What is certain about the history of tea is that its production evolved over the course of several centuries in China, that it was a food and a medicine before it was a beverage and that it was ground and whisked before it was steeped. These dramatic changes in tea consumption took place over the Tang, Song and Ming dynasties before tea as we know it spread outside China.

During the Tang Dynasty (618–907 CE), tea was primarily prepared as a decoction from compressed bricks of tea. Pieces of the bricks were ground, boiled and served with a pinch of salt. The most famous book on tea from this time, *The Classic of Tea* by Lu Yu, describes the meticulous methods of tea preparation and the dedicated wares used with them at the time.

During the Song Dynasty (960–1279 CE), tea bricks were ground and whisked in a bowl with heated water rather than boiled. It was during this time that tea preparation gained in popularity in Japan. This remains the most famous preparation method in Japan today; the basis of the Japanese tea ceremony is whisked green tea, known as matcha.

During the Ming Dynasty (1368–1644 CE), loose leaf tea and methods of preparation that are more recognisable to us today became widespread, and green tea, fermented tea

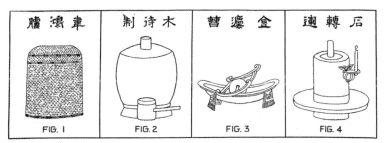

UTENSILS USED IN THE PREPARATION OF TEA IN THE TIME OF LU YU

Fig. 1 is a bamboo basket for firing tea. Fig. 2 is an anvil made of wood and an iron mallet to mould the tea into cakes. Fig. 3 is an iron grinding boat. Fig. 4 is a stone grinding mill.

41

茶經卷上

唐 竟陵陸羽鴻漸著

明 新安汪士賢 校

一之源

茶者南方之嘉木也一尺二尺迺至數十尺其巴山峽川有兩人合抱者伐而掇之其樹如瓜蘆葉如梔子花如白薔薇實如栟櫚葉如丁香根如胡桃瓜蘆木出廣州似茶至苦澀栟櫚蒲葵之屬其子似茶胡桃與茶根皆下孕兆至瓦礫苗木上抽其字或從草或從木或草木并其字或從草當作茶其字出開元文字從木當作搽其字出

LU YU AND A PAGE OF THE *Ch'a Ching*, THE FIRST TEA BOOK, A.D. 780

and scented tea began to be produced. Towards the late Ming, the first shipments of tea left China for Western lands. Tea imports to the West during this period were sold in pharmacies and consumed mainly by the wealthy.

TEA BY SEA, CHA BY LAND

Now THAT we have an understanding of the origin of tea and of the six types of tea, let's go back to how tea spread around the globe and how the world's inhabitants enjoy it today. There is no question that tea spread around the world—we know that nearly every nation that came into contact with China's tea began to import it. Interestingly, the words that different languages around the world have for tea are related to how tea first arrived in their region.

The English word 'tea' comes from the Chinese character for tea, 茶, which has two main pronunciations in China, *te* from the Southern Min or Amoy topolect and *cha* from Mandarin and Cantonese. Each pronunciation took its own course around the world, and today many languages (English included) have a word for tea similar to *te* or to *cha* (following Hindi's *chāy*, most commonly rendered 'chai').

If tea spread to a country by land, the likely word for tea in the country's language is related to *cha*, whereas if tea spread to a country by sea, the likely word for tea in that country's language is related to *te*. This is mainly because

LANGUAGES WITH CHA WORDS		LANGUAGES WITH TE WORDS	
Chinese	*chá*	English	*tea*
Hindi	*chāy*	Spanish	*té*
Arabic	*shāy*	Indonesian	*teh*
Russian	*chay*	French	*thé*
Portuguese	*chá*	German	*tee*

te was used in China's coastal regions, specifically Fujian Province, where most tea exited the country for transport to Europe. Inland routes, most notably the Silk Road, were responsible for the spread of tea overland throughout the Middle East and Russia, where local languages have words for tea similar to *cha*.

There are a few exceptions, though—the Portuguese word for tea, *chá*, was a result of the Portuguese trading out of Macau (rather than Fujian), where *cha* was the predominant word-root for tea. The Japanese and Korean words for tea do not follow this pattern either, as both Japanese and Korean use *cha* for tea.

TEA INFUSES ENGLAND

THE ESTABLISHMENT of the tea trade with Europeans took place during the last 100 years of China's Ming Dynasty, with the Portuguese establishment of a trading base with China in Macau and the Dutch trading with China via Indonesia.

The first imports of tea into Europe, credited to the Dutch East India Company, reached Amsterdam in 1610. By the 1630s there were regular imports of tea into Europe. Because of its high price at the time, tea was consumed primarily by the aristocracy and, as mentioned earlier, when it was first introduced into Europe, tea was was sold in pharmacies and often drunk as a medicinal beverage. Records show that the bulk of tea imported into Europe during this time was green tea.

Tea was first sold to the public in London in 1657 by the coffee house Garraways. Its owner, Thomas Garraway, publicised 'tea as a healthy and beneficial drink'.[7] Over the following decades the sale of tea spread to the coffee houses of London which, in addition to tea and coffee, also sold

NAMIDDAG *L'APRESDINEE*

Nú zich met Thee verfrist indien de hitte u plaagt
Zo raakt die hitte door een heter hitte aen 't Koelen
Of krupt de koude uvel gaat 't lijf met Joffie spoelen
Met zulk gezelschap dat Namiddaags u behaagt

Theodorus Danckerts Excudit.   *P: v d Berge Inv: et Fecit.*

chocolate—the three exotic indulgences of the day. The coffee houses were frequented by middle- and upper-class men; women were not permitted inside.

The growth in the popularity and the quality of tea in Britain were hampered by taxes: tea was taxed in its liquid form from 1660 to 1689,[8] which led to coffee houses preparing batches of tea in bulk each morning to be reheated through the day as it was sold. The tax system was changed in 1689 to tax the dry leaf, and thus the quality of tea sold in coffee houses greatly improved as the tea could be made to order.

Catherine of Braganza is credited with sparking the trend of tea consumption among the British. A Portuguese princess already accustomed to drinking tea among the Portuguese elite, Catherine married Charles II in 1662. A chest of tea and the city of Bombay (now Mumbai) in India were included in her dowry to Charles.

Catherine's love of tea quickly spread to the women of the royal court, to aristocratic circles and to the wealthier classes of England. More and more women began taking tea in their homes, following the queen's habit. It was during this time that porcelain tea-ware, also popularised by Catherine, became fashionable.

Having been hampered by its lack of success in setting up a trading base with China, the English East India Company imported the first shipments of tea to England in the

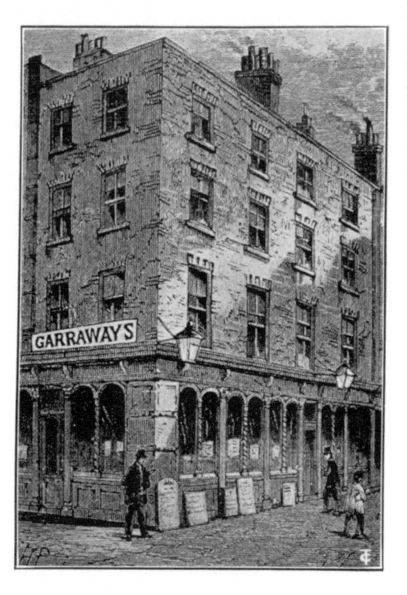

1660s. Up till then all tea had arrived in England by way of the Dutch East India Company.

The late seventeenth century saw a gradual rise in tea consumption among wealthy families according to household records from the time.[9] In the first two decades of the eighteenth century Thomas Twinings built a successful business empire selling dry leaves to the people of London for preparation at home. Twinings was also the first to introduce the practice of blending teas. Twinings' shop at 216 Strand still stands to this day.

In the 1720s black tea began to overtake green tea in popularity. It is thought that the widespread adulteration of green teas, by the adding of leaves from other plants to increase profits and by the adding of chemicals to achieve the 'correct' colour of infusion, led to a decrease in the consumption of green tea and to an increase in that of black tea. The British Parliament sought to end this practice by passing the Adulteration of Tea Act in 1776 which levied a fine on anyone caught selling adulterated tea in an inspection.

It is thought that the practice of adding milk and sugar to tea also came into fashion during the 1720s. There are a number of explanations for this. Some historians say that it was a result of experimentation and that, because it rounded out the taste of over-steeped black tea and added a nutritional boost to the drink, the practice spread. Others say that milk was added to delicate porcelain tea-ware

Ph. Mercier Pinx.ᵗ   Publish'd according to Act of Parliament Jan.ᵗ 1760   Rich. Houston Fecit.

Just risen from Repose fair Delia see;   **MORNING.**   Thus does the Nymph her Morning hours waste;

Sipping with sweet Joy her favorite Tea;   And smiles indulgent on the glad Repast.

London, Printed for Robᵗ Sayer opposite Fetter Lane Fleet Street. Price 1 6.ᵈ before the tea was poured in order to temper the heat of the tea to prevent the ware from breaking.

By 1750 imports of tea by the English East India Company had reached nearly five million pounds.[10] Because of the high duty levied on teas, smuggling was rampant. Some historians estimate that in the latter part of the eighteenth century more tea was imported illegally than legally. Tea merchants acting legally pressurised the government to take action, and in 1785 the duty on tea was reduced enough to destroy the smuggling trade.[11] This resulted in a reduction in the price of tea so that it became available to most people.

Around 1760, with the new machines and industrial practices of the Industrial Revolution, workers toiled long hours in factories, and tea was there to revive them. Ranit Bhuyan of the London Tea History Association explained to me that the Industrial Revolution marked the beginning of the tea break, which owners and managers provided to workers in order to pressurise them to work longer hours while maintaining acceptable levels of productivity. Tea was now a beverage enjoyed by the working class.

The Industrial Revolution led to widespread pollution and overcrowded cities, which in turn led to the spread of disease. Drinking water needed to be boiled so as to be safe for consumption. How better to enhance the flavour of water than to steep tea in it?

The British were reliant on the Chinese for tea, but there was little that the Chinese desired from the British but for silver—that is, until they were introduced to opium. The opium trade grew from the the early nineteenth century, and China's efforts to stop its import by making it illegal led to the First Opium War in 1839. The war ended in defeat for the Chinese in 1842: Hong Kong was ceded to the British, trading posts were established along China's coast and the opium trade continued.

Intent on breaking China's monopoly on tea production, the British sought to produce their own tea in their colonies. In 1848 the British East India Company employed the Scottish botanist Robert Fortune to steal tea plants from China, which he did successfully, apparently while in disguise.

It was the discovery of native tea plants in India, however, that proved to be the most important development in the move towards freedom from the Chinese monopoly on tea. In the nineteenth century, the British established commercial tea production across India in Assam, the Nilgiris and Darjeeling.

CHINESE TEA CULTURE

WE LEFT off our story of tea in China in the Ming Dynasty and the proliferation of loose leaf tea around the time that tea spread to Europe. As tea consumption spread around the globe, China retained its monopoly on tea production. Today, China remains the world's top tea exporter, producing a staggering 35 per cent of the world's tea.[12]

As early as the Song Dynasty, tea was considered one of the 'seven necessities' to begin a day, along with firewood, rice, oil, salt, sauce and vinegar. Today, while most of the world's tea consumers prefer black tea, 54 per cent of tea consumed in China is green tea.[13] In China tea is most commonly taken loose in a glass thermos, and sources of hot water for tea are easy to find in train stations and airports. These thermoses typically have a small screen near the mouth to keep the leaves at bay, but the leaves remain submerged and more water is added throughout the day to the same leaves.

There also exists a strong connoisseur class of tea drinkers in China. After all, some of the highest-quality teas are

produced there. Some of the most highly sought-after teas are the first green teas produced each season. These teas are known as pre-Qing Ming teas, which means that the teas are harvested before the Qing Ming Festival. *Qing Ming* translates into English as 'tomb sweeping' and is the time of year when respect is paid to ancestors. The holiday falls at the beginning of April, around the time when the first tea buds appear on the tea plants as they come out of winter dormancy. These first harvests just before Qing Ming fetch high prices on the market and are said to be packed with nutrients that have been stored up over the winter while the plants were dormant.

Tea connoisseurs in China also seek out Pu'er teas from specific producing villages in Yunnan Province. In recent years, the village of Lao Ban Zhang has produced some of the most sought-after Pu'ers seen since the Pu'er bubble of 2007 (see page 37 and the fermented tea chapter). Pu'er tea is remarkable in that it is often pressed into shapes and aged. Properly stored, decades-old Pu'er is treated like a fine wine and is highly prized.

A tea preparation method known as *gong fu cha* which loosely translates as 'tea made with skill' is popular among tea connoisseurs in China, and increasingly abroad. Its root word, *gongfu*, is the Pinyin transliteration of *kung fu*, which refers to the famous martial art form, but both words have the same definition—to do something that takes practice, skill and patience.

An entire book could be written on the methods of *gong fu cha*, but the essence of the preparation style is that the tea leaves are steeped many times using a small amount of water each time, with a high concentration of tea leaves. In one tea-drinking session, where you may consume ten to twenty small cups of tea, you are able to experience the tea blossom, as earlier steepings are light in taste and colour, and the steepings grow in strength before subsiding completely.

Traditional *gong fu cha* requires the use of a *gaiwan*, simply a cup with a lid, typically made of porcelain, where the lid can be tilted slightly to pour out the tea while the leaves remain in the cup, or a Yi Xing teapot, which is made of a special porous clay that absorbs the tea flavours and becomes seasoned over time. Tea is decanted from either the *gaiwan* or Yi Xing pot into a small pitcher, then poured into small cups for drinking. This method is most often used for the preparation of oolong, Pu'er and other high-end teas.

Quite apart from the enjoyment that it provides, tea is an extremely important part of daily life for the Chinese, an important agricultural export and a major part of China's rich and vast cultural heritage.

JAPANESE TEA CULTURE

JAPAN HAS a rich culture of tea preparation and tea art which began hundreds of years before tea reached the West. Tea was first introduced into Japan from China by Buddhist monks who travelled back and forth between the countries. The first tea seeds grown in Japan were brought from China by monks named Kukai and Saicho in 805 CE, while the first written reference to tea in Japanese history dates back to 815 CE, when the emporer Saga was served tea by the Buddhist monk Eichu.

It wasn't until after 1211, however, when the Buddhist monk Esai returned from China and published his work *Kissa Yōjōki* ('Drinking Tea for Health') that tea became popular in Japan. Esai propagated 'Zen [Buddhism] as a teaching that could save Japan and tea as a medicine that could restore the Japanese people to health'.[14]

The Japanese tea ceremony, known as *chanoyu* (literally, 'hot water for tea'), involves much more than just hot water for tea. It is a complex ritual with hundreds of strictures governing everything from the number of guests allowed

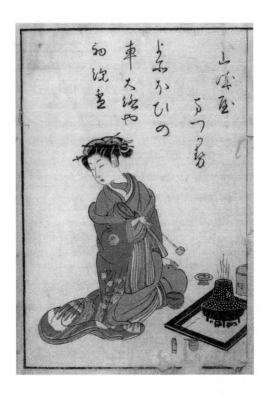

to the structure of the ceremony, the tools used to prepare and serve the tea and the hand movements involved. The ceremony is meant to be performed and experienced as a meditation. *Chanoyu* as we know it today originated in the sixteenth century, when its foundations were laid by Murata Jukō and Takeno Jōō.

The most influential figure in the development of *chanoyu* was Sen no Rikyū. Rikyū, who served as tea master for the daimyos Oda Nobunaga and Toyotomi Hideyoshi, developed many of the procedures and implements used for the tea ceremony and became well known for his mastery of tea preparation. However, Hideyoshi, overtaken by paranoia and fearing that Rikyū might poison his tea, ordered him to commit ritual suicide, or *seppuku* (suicide by disembowelment). Rikyū did so in 1591, at the age of 70, after performing a lavish final tea ceremony. During his final tea ceremony, he declared, 'Never again shall this cup, polluted by the lips of misfortune, be used by man', as he broke his cup into pieces.

A key element of the *chanoyu* is the preparation of matcha, a fine green powder made from ground tea leaves. In the ceremony, matcha powder is whisked into suspension in hot water with a bamboo whisk called a *chasen*, in a bowl, and served. Matcha is still popular today, and has seen a recent rise in popularity as it has been lauded as a healthy ingredient and is added to beverages and baked goods in cafes around the world.

Today, Japan is the world's eleventh largest producer of tea[15] and the only major producer of matcha. Ninety-eight per cent of tea products from Japan are made up of steamed green teas, a process developed in the eighteenth century by Sōen Nagatani to halt oxidation in tea leaves during processing. This led to the two styles of green tea that Japan is most famous for after matcha: sencha and gyokuro.[16]

Sencha and gyokuro are typically prepared in a side-handled teapot called a *kyusu*. This style of tea preparation is

known as *senchado*. The first leaves harvested each spring are highly sought-after and are known as *shincha*, or 'new tea'. Because Japanese green teas are steamed, they retain much of the green aroma and flavour compounds of the leaves, and are known for their vegetal, umami-packed taste. These teas are often sold according to the level of steaming they have undergone.

Today, the bulk of tea consumed in Japan is bottled green tea. However, the cultural relevance of tea has not been lost, as the recent rise in the popularity of matcha has led to a resurgence of awareness about the Japanese tea ceremony, and tea connoisseurs have much to appreciate in the loose leaf green teas being produced today.

INDIAN TEA CULTURE

TEA PRODUCTION in India was pioneered by the Singpho people, a tribe that inhabited parts of Arunachal Pradesh and Assam in India. The Singpho processed tea leaves from native tea plants which were then stored in tubes of bamboo. It is thought that the Singpho were making and drinking tea in India hundreds of years before the British commercialised production there. For a time, the British had no idea that tea plants were native to the region.

When the country was under British rule, northern India was deemed to be the perfect place for the commercial production of tea. The British were hoping to overcome the Chinese monopoly on tea. Numerous attempts were made to cultivate tea plants and tea seeds acquired from China, but most proved unsuccessful. It was the discovery of the native plants used by the Singphos in the 1820s and 1830s by Robert Bruce, his brother Charles Bruce and Lieutenant Charlton that led to the viability of a commercial crop. In his notes, Charles recounted:

I feel convinced the whole of the country is full of tea …
I found … small hills … covered with tea-plants. The
flowers of the tea on these hills are of a pleasant delicate
fragrance, unlike the smell of our other tea-plants; but the
leaves and fruit appear the same. This would be a delight-
ful place for the manufacture of tea, as the country is well
populated, has abundance of grain, and labour is cheap.[17]

Planting operations were started in the Nilgiris, Assam
and Darjeeling between the 1830s and the 1850s. The turn-
ing point came in 1887 when Britain imported more tea
from India and Sri Lanka than from China.[18] Today, India

is the world's second largest producer of tea, and its teas account for 21 per cent of the world's total production.[19]

Having successfully broken the Chinese monopoly on tea, producers in India turned inwards. To spur the growth of domestic tea consumption, the Indian Tea Association launched major marketing campaigns in the early twentieth century. The association held in-home demonstrations on tea making, set up small shops in towns and ports, and tea stalls in factories to keep workers energised, and sent tea makers to the railways to sell tea to train passengers.

This was the genesis of the *chai wallah*, or 'tea seller'. During this period, some tea makers added spices to their tea, which initially caused frustration among association officials because it allowed tea makers to get away with using less tea in their brew. But this unique Indian touch caught on and spread as tea spread, and now masala chai, or 'spiced tea', is a popular preparation of tea across India. The spices added to tea vary widely, but typically combine cardamom, cloves, cinnamon, ginger, star anise or black pepper.

Today, street stalls can be found in every Indian city at which *chai wallah*s sell cups of masala chai or simply milk tea (the same preparation without the spices). The cups are typically hastily made from clay and are thrown back to the earth after a single use. Complex networks of delivery people deliver chai to Indian offices, fuelling workers through their working day.

Masala chai is traditionally made by boiling CTC black tea and a blend of spices in a combination of milk and water. Since the early years of the twenty-first century, it has grown in popularity in India and abroad. Many Western tea and coffee outposts offer a Westernised version of this beverage by using a concentrated mix of already steeped tea and spices in milk or by steeping tea and spices in hot water and adding milk and sweeteners afterwards. A common misnomer arose when several large Western cafe chains began referring to masala tea as 'chai tea'—*chai*, of course, is the Hindi word for tea, so 'chai tea' actually means 'tea tea'.

Around 85 per cent of tea production in India is CTC black tea.[20] CTC is a production method whereby tea leaves are crushed, torn and curled using machinery. The resulting tea is made up of tiny pieces of broken tea leaves. This style of tea is destined to be used for domestic milk tea and in tea bags around the world.

Tea connoisseurs both in India and abroad are drawn to the teas of Darjeeling, which are often lauded as the champagne of teas. This production region in the foothills of the Himalayas is home to eighty-seven tea gardens and is one of the most strongly protected geographical indications in the tea world. The most sought-after teas from Darjeeling are made from the first leaves that sprout each spring, collectively called first flush teas. These leaves are processed in the 'orthodox' style, which means that the leaves are treated with more care and are not intentionally broken into fragments, as with CTC tea, leading to a more nuanced flavour profile. Despite its popularity, tea production in Darjeeling accounts for only 1 per cent of tea produced in India, which is more a testament to the sheer quantity of CTC tea produced in the country than to the lack of popularity of Darjeeling's teas.[21]

CEYLON TEAS IN LEAD PACKETS.

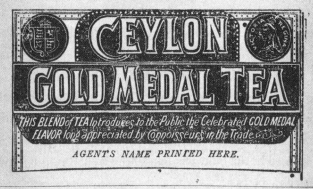

Where Vacancies may exist Agents are appointed by

THE GREAT TOWER STREET TEA COMPANY, Ld.,

LONDON: 5, Jewry Street, E.C.   PARIS: Rue de Rivoli, 204.

SRI LANKAN TEA CULTURE

Sri Lanka is a tropical island nation just off the southern tip of India, roughly the size of Ireland. Despite its size, Sri Lanka is the fourth largest tea producer in the world behind China, India and Kenya.[22] The story of tea in Sri Lanka began while it was still a British colony and was known as Ceylon. In 1824 Robert Bruce, who also cultivated tea in India, grew tea plants in the Royal Botanical Gardens in Peradeniya. It wasn't until 1867, however, that the first commercial plantation was established at Loolecondera Estate by the Scotsman James Taylor, who is known in Sri Lanka for having established the tea industry there.

Before the advent of tea, coffee had been the major crop on the island, but the entire industry was wiped out when a fungus destroyed the crop in 1869. Farmers turned to alternative crops and, following Taylor's example at Loolecondera, began planting tea. The destruction of the coffee crop in Sri Lanka ultimately led to its becoming a major force in world tea production.

Remarkably, the Sri Lankan tea industry relies heavily on smallholders for production. These are small, family-run plots of tea plants under 10 acres in size (the average plot size is 0.85 acres). The leaves are harvested by smallholders and sold to processing facilities. There are 475,000 small-holders in Sri Lanka who are responsible for producing 70 per cent of the country's tea.[23]

Ninety-five per cent of the tea produced in Sri Lanka is orthodox black tea,[24] but in recent years more and more producers have been experimenting with the production of speciality teas such as white silver tips. Orthodox black teas grown in Sri Lanka are classified by elevation and region, with teas from the highest elevations fetching the highest prices on the market. Tea grown below 600 metres is clas-sified as 'low country', that produced between 600 metres and 1,200 metres as 'mid-country' and that produced above 1,200 metres as 'up-country' or 'high country'.

The major producing regions—Kandy, Nuwara Eliya, Uda Pussellawa, Uva, Dimbula, Sabaragamuwa and Ruhuna—are concentrated in the central highland and southern inland parts of the island. Nuwara Eliya, which has highest average elevation of all of the producing regions in Sri Lanka, produces some of the most sought-after teas. Despite producing so much tea, Sri Lanka exports an astounding 95 per cent of it![25]

BRITISH TEA CULTURE

WE PAUSED on our journey with afternoon tea in the 1840s, around the time that commercial tea production began in India. It was this production that broke China's monopoly in 1887, when for the first time the British imported more tea from its own colonies (India and Sri Lanka).

The concept of 'afternoon tea' is credited to Anna, the seventh Duchess of Bedford, and the practice spread among the British upper class in the 1830s and 1840s. Afternoon tea is a light meal made up of small snacks and sweets taken with tea late in the afternoon, before dinner. Afternoon tea eventually spread to all social classes, and became an important social occasion. Upmarket afternoon teas are still taken in Britain and in high-end hotels around the world today where scones and other sweets, along with finger sandwiches, are served with a selection of teas.

In the Victorian era, a certain level of etiquette was required, whether in serving or in being a guest at an afternoon tea. From the invitations to the dress code, to the tea-wares, to the way the tea was stirred, there was a 'proper'

EMPIRE TEA
from
INDIA, CEYLON
& EAST AFRICA
*Every man, woman & child in the
United Kingdom drinks on the
average 5 cups of tea a day*
SEE THAT YOUR TEA IS LABELLED
"GUARANTEED EMPIRE GROWN"

EMPIRE TEA
from
INDIA, CEYLON
& EAST AFRICA
*The Empire grows enough tea to
supply all the Empire's needs
& to suit every taste & purse*
SEE THAT YOUR TEA IS LABELLED
"GUARANTEED EMPIRE GROWN"

Effective Posters Distributed by the Empire Marketing Board in the United Kingdom

way to do it. Today there are tea houses that give classes on tea etiquette.

The concept of 'high tea' originated as a working-class evening meal, for teatime had to wait until after work was over. High tea often involved heavy foods and was more of a tea-dinner, though the concept is often confused with afternoon tea. The name is thought to have derived from the fact that high tea was enjoyed at a high table, whereas afternoon tea was taken at a lower table. With the advent of afternoon tea and high tea, tea drinking became an event or a social institution—tea was clearly much more than just a beverage.

Until the 1950s, all tea consumed in Britain was prepared as loose leaves. In 1953 Tetley introduced tea bags to the market. In the early 1960s they were used by only 3 per cent of tea drinkers, but today nearly 96 per cent of the British tea market is made up of tea bags.[26] Nearly all of the tea consumed in Britain is black tea, often blends of East African and Assam teas.

There is an ongoing debate among passionate tea drinkers in Britain as to whether milk should be added to the cup before or after the tea is poured. Either way, it is standard to associate taste with colour, in terms of the strength of the steep and the amount of added milk. The strongest and darkest of brews, even after milk is added, is informally referred to as 'builder's tea', a reference to the strong brew preferred by blue-collar workers.

Today, tea is typically taken multiple times a day in a mug with a tea bag. Hot water is heated up in an electric kettle and poured into the mug over the tea bag. In some countries, such as the United States, a kettle refers to a vessel used to boil water on the stove, whereas in Britain a kettle is typically a vessel that plugs into an electric socket. The latter type quickly converts electricity to heat and brings water to a rolling boil in 3–5 minutes. It has been observed that, after popular television shows in the United Kingdom, the power grid sees surges of up to 3 gigawatts (depending on the popularity of the show), as the audience goes to make their post-show tea.[27]

In 1999 a tea plantation was established at Tregothnan in Cornwall, with 30 acres of land under cultivation and

120,000 tea plants. The first ever British-grown tea produced there was sold in 2005.

Currently, the United Kingdom ranks third in the world for tea consumption per capita.[28] British tea consumption amounts to an astounding 60.2 billion[29] cups of tea per year. The beverage is lauded for solving all of Britain's problems, great or small.

MOROCCAN TEA CULTURE

IN MOROCCO, which ranks sixth in the world for tea consumption per capita,[30] there is a unique tea preparation that is a major cultural fixture for Moroccans and a central tenet of Moroccan hospitality.

The core of Moroccan tea culture is mint tea, often referred to as Maghrebi mint tea or Touareg tea. Mint tea is prepared for guests and is drunk throughout the day by the Moroccan people. The tea is prepared by steeping Chinese gunpowder green tea with sprigs of fresh spearmint in a teapot. Copious amounts of sugar are added to the infusion and the tea is then poured from a height into small glass cups so as to create foam on the surface. The tea is usually served three times in succession and, because the leaves remain in the pot, the flavour changes with each successive brew, giving rise to the famous Moroccan tea proverb:

> The first glass is as bitter as life,
> The second glass is as strong as love,
> The third glass is as gentle as death.

Historians argue as to how this distinct tea culture came about. Some attribute the introduction of tea to Morocco to the Berbers, while others hold that tea arrived in the area in the twelfth century. Regardless, tea in Morocco remains a staple and its unique preparation of tea has spread across North Africa.

A traditional Moroccan tea set is made up of an ornate silver teapot, several glasses (often without handles) and a silver tray. In the West, this style of tea is often referred to simply as 'Moroccan mint tea' and is sold in loose form as a mixture of gunpowder green tea and dried mint leaves.

AMERICAN TEA CULTURE

LIKE BRITAIN, the American colonies received their first shipments of tea from the Dutch East India Company in the middle of the seventeenth century. Wealthy colonists adopted the English tea culture, holding afternoon teas which were served using beautiful wares. As in Britain, tea spread to all classes and throughout the colony. William Penn is credited with bringing tea to Philadelphia, which he founded in 1682.

Boston, New York and Philadelphia became the key ports for importing tea that was controlled by the British, for the American colonies were still under British rule at the time. A series of taxes imposed on the importation of tea by the British led to growing discontent among the American colonists, who were beginning to resist being taxed while not having any elected representation of their own in the British Parliament.

When the British East India Company, stuck with a surplus of tea and near financial collapse was granted permission by Parliament to export tea directly to the

American colonies in 1773, the discontent among colonists grew to a fervour. On 16 December 1773 colonists dressed as Native Americans boarded ships filled with tea in Boston harbour and dumped 90,000 pounds of tea into the harbour. This event became known as the Boston Tea Party.

Similar events took place across the American colonies, and the consumption of tea became an unpatriotic act. These events helped to spark the American Revolutionary War, which ended on 3 September 1783, with the signing of the Treaty of Paris which recognised the sovereignty of the United States. It is thought that these events are the reason why the United States is more of a coffee-drinking nation to this day. However, even though it was one of the events leading up to the war, and though it was seen as unpatriotic at the time, tea consumption never fully died out. After the war, Americans, who were now free to trade with whomever they wanted, were able to import tea directly from China.

During the 1840s and 1850s American merchants pioneered a new type of ship that could haul bulk goods overseas more quickly than had previously been possible: the clipper ship. Clippers reduced the shipping time from ten to fifteen months to around 100 days,[31] which allowed new tea harvests from China to be rushed to market and to arrive fresh.

Our story of tea has so far revolved around loose leaf tea. It wasn't until the early twentieth century that the tea bag entered the scene in the United States. Roberta C. Lawson

THE DESTRUCTION OF TEA AT BOSTON HARBOR.

and Mary McLaren, two women from Milwaukee, Wisconsin, hold the first patent for the tea bag, but they are largely unknown in the tea world, so it seems that they were unable to bring their invention to market. It wasn't until Thomas Sullivan, a tea merchant from New York, began sending tea samples in silk bags to potential customers in 1908 that the idea took hold. Sullivan had used silk bags to store the samples for shipping and had not intended them to be steeped directly, so it is often said that he invented the tea bag accidentally. While it may have been an accident, he was credited with their rise in popularity.

The United States has championed the use of flavours and scents in tea which has led to increased access to tea and to a rise in speciality tea sales in the twenty-first century. The bulk of tea sold in the United States is in the form of tea bags and bottled tea. The most common preparation is iced tea, made from black tea bags and heavily sweetened. It is known as 'sweet tea' in the southern United States, where the sugar content is often so high that it approaches the sugar level of a soft drink. Bottled tea is often both sweetened and flavoured, but a few new entrants to the market are touting pure tea. Tea connoisseurship has recently risen in popularity, and self-proclaimed 'tea nerds' have added a tea ritual to their daily lives.

In politics tea saw a resurgence in the 2010s following the creation of the Tea Party movement in 2009, a conservative Republican (and not very popular) movement aimed at reducing the size of the US government and centred on right-wing populist ideas.

The United States is not usually seen as a tea-producing nation, although an estate in South Carolina has called itself the only US tea plantation for years. The past decade has seen the growth of a number of tea-growing operations, with the majority of these in Hawaii.

According to the Tea Association of the United States, over 158 million Americans currently drink tea each day.[32] Eighty per cent of the tea sold in the United States is black tea and 16 per cent green tea.

PREPARING TEA

NOW THAT we've journeyed far and wide, and have an understanding of what tea is and where it came from, the next logical step is to learn the proper way to prepare it—after all, this is why we love tea.

A steeped cup of tea is more than 98 per cent water, so it follows that we must begin with a good, clean water source. Water is often described as 'the mother of tea' and the nuances of a good tea can be lost if the tap water has been treated with chlorine or chloramine. Any off-tastes or aromas present in the water before tea is steeped in it will undoubtedly still be present after steeping. The use of a charcoal water filter, or bottled spring water, will ensure a good water source to start with.

Moving on to the tea leaves, I will assume that if you are reading up to this point you'll be using loose leaf tea. After all, tea bags have been around for only a brief moment of time when you take into account all of tea history. If not, I urge you to give loose leaf tea a chance. Get yourself some beautiful, full, unbroken tea leaves!

A GROUP OF ENGLISH TEA-TASTING REQUISITES

No. 1—Tea-tasting kettle; No. 2—Whistling gas kettle; No. 3—Tea-testing scales; No. 4—Tea-tasting clock; No. 5—Infusing pot; No. 6—Tasting cup; No 7—Tea-tasting spittoon; No. 8—Tea-tasting spoons.

Preparing tea need not be a complex operation. The preparation of a delicious cup of tea depends on the proper proportion of tea leaves to hot water and time.

There is no perfect way to prepare tea, as each person prefers their tea to be brewed to a strength that they find acceptable. We can, however, explore the variables that we can control when preparing tea so that we achieve the intended strength of brew.

The following instructions are based on a recommended 1 gram of tea for each 50 millilitres of water. Because loose leaf tea leaves vary in size and shape, it is nearly impossible to measure them out by volume—yes, I'm saying that *tea*spoons serve no valid purpose here. But I'm not advocating the use of scales every time you want to make a cup of tea. This chapter should be used as a guide to help you develop your own personal tea style, and after some practice you'll be able to estimate how much tea to use with no problem.

When steeping tea, the effects of water temperature and steep time on the beverage are inversely correlated. This means that, for a preferred steep time and water temperature to prepare an infusion of a particular strength, a slight increase in the steep time and a decrease in the water temperature will yield a similar result. Likewise, a decrease in the steep time and an increase in the water temperature will also yield a similar result.

In general, green and yellow teas produce the best-tasting tea steeped at lower temperatures (well under boiling) and with steep times between 30 and 90 seconds. Japanese green teas (or any other green teas that have been steamed) should be steeped closer to the short end of the range and at a temperature between 60°C and 70°C (140–160°F), though most green and yellow teas can produce a nice result between 60°C and 80°C (140–180°F). If you have ever experienced a green tea that was so bitter and astringent that you had to add honey or sugar to it, that green tea fell victim to either too long a steep time or too hot a steep temperature. In my experience, most people who have an unfavourable opinion of green tea change their minds once they have had a properly prepared green tea.

Next up are white teas. I like to steep white teas in hot water anywhere from 80°C to 96°C (180–205°F). A few schools of thought hold that white teas should be steeped at a much lower temperature, but I find the resulting brew watery. I like to steep white teas hard and long, anywhere from 1 to 2 minutes.

Because oolong is such a diverse category, spanning tea styles that vary in the degree of oxidation, less oxidised (greener) oolongs should be steeped for a shorter time, and more oxidised (browner) oolongs for a longer time. While they can be steeped anywhere between 80°C and 96°C (180–205°F) to provide a nice-tasting brew, I like to steep mine at 90°C (195°F) and to vary the time depending on the tea.

I steep black teas anywhere from 90°C to 99°C (195–210°F) and between 1 and 2 minutes. Many tea companies recommend that black teas be steeped for 3–5 minutes. While that is all right if you want to mute the resulting bitter brew with milk and sugar, I find that if you stop the steeping process at around the 2-minute mark, you will get a completely different experience and be able to taste a sweetness in the tea.

Note that this works only for high-quality loose leaf teas; trying this out with a tea bag will not yield the same results. Tea bags are typically filled with the tiniest bits of black tea available so that they steep almost instantly; they are also products of blending so that they taste the same each time.

Finally, fermented teas. Teas from this diverse category, regardless of their level of fermentation, can typically be steeped at or near boiling, with steep times ranging from 30 to 90 seconds, depending on the tea. Younger and less fermented teas such as sheng Pu'er should be steeped closer to 30 seconds, while older and more fermented teas, as well as shu Pu'er, can be steeped for longer.

Choosing a time for steeping loose leaf tea is a skill, as the only way to measure surface area is with your eyes. If the tea leaves are broken—and have a greater surface area—they will steep more quickly than the same leaves in unbroken form. This is something that you will learn over time by observing the leaves and practising the art and science of steeping tea. Another thing you'll learn with practice is the ability to tell when a tea has finished steeping either by the appearance of the leaves or by the aroma of the infusion.

If you are having trouble producing a palatable infusion from your tea, here are a few rules of thumb. For best results change only one variable at a time, and experiment in the order listed.

If your tea is too strong:

☞ decrease the steep time;
☞ use less tea; or
☞ decrease the steep temperature.

If your tea is too weak:

☞ increase the steep time;

☞ use more tea; or

☞ increase the water temperature.

Remember that the sweet spot for each tea will vary, so experiment often. Sometimes the best way to find that spot is to over-steep the tea on purpose, in order to find its limits and then take it back a notch. Tea preparation is not an act governed by strict rules; the methods outlined here are simply provided as a starting point for experimentation.

Notice that I've not yet mentioned any sort of steeping vessel. That is because it doesn't matter! As long as the leaves are in contact with water at the prescribed temperature for the prescribed time and you can remove the leaves from the water after this time, you're good. That said, there are many tea-wares and accessories on the market to help you accomplish this.

Two simple contraptions that have made their way into my kitchen are an infuser basket and a *gaiwan*. The infuser basket is a large cup-shaped mesh device that holds tea leaves and sits right inside a mug. The important thing here is that it is large, and takes up the interior space of the mug. This allows the leaves room to unfurl as they steep, enabling the water to come into contact with all sides of each leaf and ensuring an even brew. This device is also

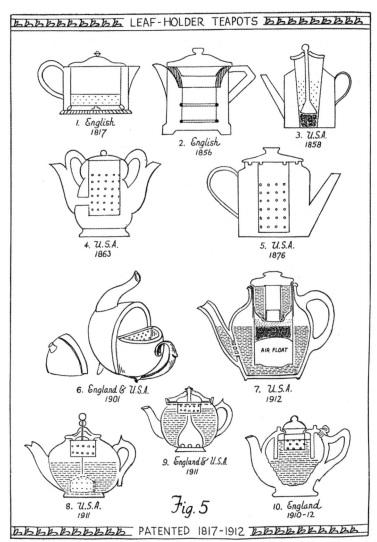

1. *English* 1817

2. *English* 1856

3. *U.S.A.* 1858

4. *U.S.A.* 1863

5. *U.S.A.* 1876

6. *England & U.S.A.* 1901

7. *U.S.A.* 1912

AIR FLOAT

8. *U.S.A.* 1911

9. *England & U.S.A.* 1911

10. *England* 1910-12

Fig. 5

PATENTED 1817-1912

VARIOUS ENGLISH AND AMERICAN PATENT INSET INFUSER TEAPOTS

1. Ogle's tea or coffee biggin. 2. Suspended strainer bag. 3. Leaf Squeezer. 4. Dual strength. 5. Removable leaf basket, attached to lid. 6. "S.Y.P." tip-over pot. 7. The "London Tea Bob." 8. Raisable leaf holder. 9. Air-valve leaf separator. 10. The "Anti-Tannic" air-valve tea infuser.

simple because I can remove it from the mug once my steep time has elapsed. Stay away from small infuser balls and gimmicky tea infuser devices—those leaves need room to expand!

The *gaiwan* is an ingenious device from China, literally a 'cup with lid', and it is just that, a cup with a lid that sits on a saucer. Leaves and water are put into the cup which is covered with the lid. When the tea is ready to drink, you tip the lid slightly, holding back the leaves and pour the water out into a drinking vessel.

Our story is nearly complete. We now know what tea is, where it comes from, how it's made and how it has enraptured people around the world with its brew. Let us now touch on how it affects our bodies once we consume it.

TEA AND HEALTH

THE GROWTH of the tea market in recent years can almost entirely be attributed to the marketing of tea as a healthy beverage. Countless studies have zeroed in on complex tea chemicals and their impact on the body, and, as tea's popularity increases, there will be more studies on tea and health and we'll learn more about our beloved brew.

Ideally, people should drink tea because they like it, rather than in the hope that it will be a cure-all. Tea may have started out as a medicine, and one day we may learn enough about its bioactive properties to use compounds within it as a medicine, but this book is about the philosophy of tea—and tea appreciation. Nevertheless, let's look at what we know today about tea and health.

Before we dive into what recent studies are telling us, consider that replacing fizzy, sugary beverages in our diet with tea is a healthy choice, as it reduces our sugar intake. We know that consuming water is good for our bodies, and tea is 98 per cent water, so tea has that going for it too.

We also know that all true teas contain caffeine, so watch your tea intake if you are sensitive to caffeine. There is no good way to remove caffeine from tea leaves without also removing some of their flavour, so you will rarely see the best teas decaffeinated.

Tea also contains L-theanine, an amino acid proven to promote relaxation. It is thought that L-theanine, in conjunction with caffeine, promotes a sense of mindful alertness.

And then there is matcha, which is often touted as the healthiest tea because, when you drink matcha, you are consuming the tea leaves themselves, ground into a fine powder that is whisked into suspension in the water. So, if there is any benefit to drinking tea, there is a good chance that the benefit is enhanced by consuming tea leaves in the form of matcha.

Let us take a look at the latest studies on the effect of tea on cancer, heart health and weight loss, as tea has often been claimed to have an effect on these. The following discussion should be taken with a pinch of salt, as there are many contradictory studies on each topic, and marketing should be separated from fact when buying tea. I've done my best to find research on each topic that provides an overview of recent studies. None of this is medical advice. It is simply a summary of what recent scientific studies have told us.

Tea and Cancer Prevention

Most studies on tea and cancer have focused on green tea, specifically the polyphenol epigallocatechin gallate (ECGC). Of all tea types, green tea has the highest ECGC content. But all teas have polyphenols, and teas other than green tea and polyphenols other than ECGC are now being studied. These polyphenols have exhibited antioxidant activity in many studies and are being investigated for their potential ability to prevent or to treat cancer. After reviewing fifty studies on the topic of tea and cancer risk since 2006, the United States' National Cancer Institute stated that 'the results of these studies have often been inconsistent, but some have linked tea consumption to reduced risks of cancers of the colon, breast, ovary, prostate, and lung'.[33] However, a panel of experts from the International Agency for Research on Cancer reviewed a number of recent studies and concluded that drinking hot beverages such as tea is 'probably carcino-genic' to humans, citing the risk of oesophageal cancer.[34] It is important to note that the latter panel concluded that the risk pertains to all beverages served in excess of 140°F, while tea is often taken below this temperature.

Tea and Heart Health

A 2014 review of seven studies that included 8,459 cases of coronary heart disease found that an increase in consump-tion of three cups of tea per day saw a reduced risk in heart disease of 27 per cent. It is important to note, though, that the results of the individual studies varied greatly according to the sex and ethnic backgrounds of those studied, as well as the types of tea consumed.[35]

Tea and Weight Loss

Tea has been marketed for years as a beverage that promotes weight loss. Just search for 'weight loss tea' on the internet. A number of complex weight loss pathways related to tea consumption are being studied, most of them based on the possibility that tea may be able to dissolve lipids (fat) and have a beneficial effect on our gut microbiome.

There are hundreds of studies on these and other more complex topics. A 2012 review of thirty-eight clinical studies on tea consumption and weight loss revealed that over 80 per cent of the studies demonstrated that tea consumption beneficially affected weight loss outcomes,[36] while another review in 2018 of fifteen recent studies concluded that tea polyphenols 'exhibit measurable weight-loss properties in a large majority of studies'.[37]

That sounds like good news, but while these studies exhibited positive results it's important to note how positive they actually are. Some studies produced a result that is just measurable, while others showed a more positive one, but a minority of studies found no conclusive results at all. So there is still work to be done before we are able to understand the impact that tea can have on weight management.

There is a pattern developing; there seems to be the potential for tea to have a positive impact on our health, but there is much still to be learned. So—we should drink tea because we like it, not in the hope that we will lose weight and be super-healthy. It's delicious, and there's a whole range of teas to try—your tea journey awaits you!

CHINESE WOMAN GATHERING TEA.——FROM A DRAWING BY A CHINESE ARTIST.

FURTHER READING

Tony Gebely, *Tea: A User's Guide* (Brunswick, MD: Eggs and
Toast Media, 2016)

Erling Hoh and Victor H. Mair, *The True History of Tea*
(London: Thames & Hudson, 2009)

Jane Pettigrew and Bruce Richardson, *A Social History of
Tea: Tea's Influence on Commerce, Culture & Community*
(Danville, KY: Benjamin Press, 2013)

Erika Rappaport, *A Thirst for Empire: How Tea Shaped the
Modern World* (Princeton, NJ: Princeton University Press,
2019)

Jinghong Zhang, *Puer Tea: Ancient Caravans and Urban Chic*
(Washington, D.C.: University of Washington Press, 2013)

NOTES

1 'FAOSTAT Gateway', Food and Agriculture Organization of the United Nations, http://faostat3.fao.org/home/index.html, accessed 5 March 2019.

2 Dan Bolton, 'China Remains the World's Top Tea Exporter', *World Tea News*, 28 January 2019, https://worldteanews .com/market-trends-data-and-insights/china-remains-the -worlds-top-tea-exporter, accessed 22 February 2019.

3 Mary Lou Heiss and Robert J. Heiss, *The Story of Tea* (Berkeley, CA: Ten Speed Press, 2007), 74.

4 'FAOSTAT Gateway'.

5 Erling Hoh and Victor H. Mair, *The True History of Tea* (London: Thames & Hudson, 2009), 24.

6 Houyuan Lu, Jianping Zhang, Yimin Yang et al., 'Earliest Tea as Evidence for One Branch of the Silk Road across the Tibetan Plateau', *Nature*, 7 January 2016, https://www .nature.com/articles/srep18955, accessed 22 February 2019.

7 Jane Pettigrew and Bruce Richardson, *A Social History of Tea* (Danville, KY: Benjamin Press, 2013), 23.

8 'A Social History of the Nation's Favourite Drink', UK Tea
   & Infusions Association, http://www.tea.co.uk/a-social
   -history, accessed 22 February 2019.

9 Pettigrew and Richardson. *A Social History of Tea*, 28.

10 'East India Company', UK Tea & Infusions Association,
   https://www.tea.co.uk/east-india-company, accessed 22
   February 2019.

11 'A Social History of the Nation's Favourite Drink', UK Tea
   & Infusions Association, http://www.tea.co.uk/a-social
   -history, accessed 22 February 2019.

12 Bolton, 'China Remains the World's Top Tea Exporter',
   https://worldteanews.com/market-trends-data-and
   -insights/china-remains-the-worlds-top-tea-exporter,
   accessed 4 February, 2019.

13 Intergovernmental Group on Tea, *Report of the Working
   Group on Global Tea Market Analysis and Promotion*,
   http://www.fao.org/fileadmin/templates/est/COMM_
   MARKETS_MONITORING/Tea/Intersessional_2017/
   ISM-17-3-GlobalMktAnalysis_Promotion.docx, accessed
   22 February 2019.

14 Hoh and Mair, *The True History of Tea*, 85.

15 'FAOSTAT Gateway'.

16 Liang Chen, Zeno Apostolides and Zong-Mao Chen,
   Global Tea Breeding Achievements (Hangzhou: Zhejiang
   University Press, 2012), 247, 248.

17 Robert Bruce, 'Mr. Bruce's Report on Assam Tea',
   Chambers Edinburgh Journal, 25 January 1840, https://web

.archive.org/web/20061220204732/http:/liyn-an.com/
tea_room/bruce, accessed 22 February 2019.

18 K. C. Willson and M. N. Clifford, *Tea: Cultivation to Consumption* (Dordrecht: Springer, 1992), 5.

19 Bolton, 'China Remains the World's Top Tea Exporter'.

20 Chen, Apostolides and Chen, *Global Tea Breeding Achievements*, 74.

21 Baruah Pradip, 'Tea Drinking: Origin, Perceptions, Habits with Special Reference to Assam, its Tribes, and the Role of Tocklai', *Science and Culture*, 77, nos. 9–10 (2011), 365–72.

22 'FAOSTAT Gateway'.

23 Mohamed Esham, Rohitha Rosairo and Aw Wijeratne, *Future of Work for Tea Smallholders in Sri Lanka* (Colombo: International Labour Association, 2018), https://www.ilo.org/wcmsp5/groups/public/---asia/ ---ro-bangkok/---ilo-colombo/documents/publication/ wcms_654641.pdf, accessed 22 February 2019.

24 Chen, Apostolides and Chen, *Global Tea Breeding Achievements*, 125.

25 Chen, Apostolides and Chen, *Global Tea Breeding Achievements*, 130.

26 'Tea Glossary and FAQ's', UK Tea & Infusions Association, https://www.tea.co.uk/tea-faqs, accessed 22 February 2019.

27 'Tea Time in Britain Causes Predictable, Massive Surge in Electricity Demand', Geek.com. 7 January 2013, https:// www.geek.com/geek-cetera/tea-time-in-britain-causes

-predictable-massive-surge-in-electricity-demand-1535023, accessed 22 February 2019.

28 'Annual Per Capita Tea Consumption Worldwide as of 2016, by Leading Countries (in Pounds)', Statista, https://www .statista.com/statistics/507950/global-per-capita-tea -consumption-by-country, accessed 22 February 2019.

29 'Tea Glossary and FAQ's'.

30 'Annual Per Capita Tea Consumption Worldwide as of 2016'.

31 Pettigrew and Richardson, *A Social History of Tea*, 109, 111.

32 Intergovernmental Group on Tea, *Report of the Working Group on Global Tea Market Analysis and Promotion*.

33 'Tea and Cancer Prevention', National Cancer Institute, https://www.cancer.gov/about-cancer/causes-prevention/ risk/diet/tea-fact-sheet, accessed 22 February 2019.

34 International Agency for Research on Cancer, World Health Organization, 'IARC Monographs Evaluate Drinking Coffee, Maté, and Very Hot Beverages', Press Release No. 244, 15 June 2016, https://www.iarc.fr/wp-content/ uploads/2018/07/pr244_E.pdf, accessed 22 February 2019.

35 Chi Zhang, Ying-Yi Qin, Xin Wei, et al., 'Tea Consumption and Risk of Cardiovascular Outcomes and Total Mortality: A Systematic Review and Meta-analysis of Prospective Observational Studies', *European Journal of Epidemiology*, 30, no. 2 (2014): 103–13. doi:10. 1007/s10654-014-9960-x.

36 Selena Ahmed, 'Review of the Clinical Evidence on Tea Consumption and Weight Loss', in Victor R. Preedy

(ed.), *Tea in Health and Disease Prevention*, 493–508. doi:10.1016/b978-0-12-384937-3.00041-0.

37 Dylan O'Neill Rothenberg, Caibi Zhou and Lingyun Zhang, 'A Review on the Weight-Loss Effects of Oxidized Tea Polyphenols', *Molecules*, 23, no. 5 (2018), 1176. doi:10.3390/molecules23051176.

LIST OF ILLUSTRATIONS

All images from the collections of the British Library unless otherwise stated.

Also available in this series

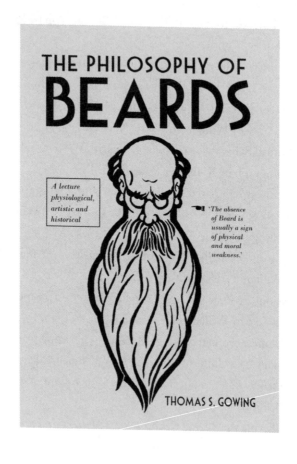

THE PHILOSOPHY OF
BEARDS

A lecture
physiological,
artistic and
historical

'The absence
of Beard is
usually a sign
of physical
and moral
weakness.'

THOMAS S. GOWING

THE PHILOSOPHY OF
COFFEE

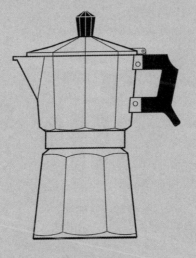

BRIAN WILLIAMS

THE PHILOSOPHY OF
WINE

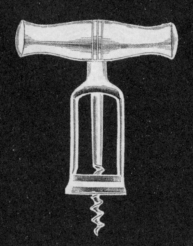

RUTH BALL